SCHIRMER'S LIBRARY
OF MUSICAL CLASSICS

Vol. 1599

T0210369

JOHANNES BRAHMS

Op. 10

Four Ballades

For the Piano

G. SCHIRMER, Inc.

DISTRIBUTED BY

HAL•LEONARD®
CORPORATION
7777 W. BLUEMOUND RD. P.O. BOX 13819 MILWAUKEE, WI 53213

Printed in the U. S. A.

Four Ballades

Johannes Brahms, Op.10

After the Scottish Ballad "Edward"

1

2

Molto staccato e leggiero

3
Intermezzo

14

4

Andante con moto

Più lento

Col intimissimo sentimento ma senza troppo marcare la Melodia